Come to the Castle!

A Visit to a Castle in Thirteenth-Century England

By Linda Ashman  Illuminated by S. D. Schindler

Rb.
Flash
Point

ROARING BROOK PRESS
NEW YORK

The Earl of Daftwood

Welcome to my castle—
How exquisite, lavish, grand!
So much land in my dominion;
So much staff at my command!

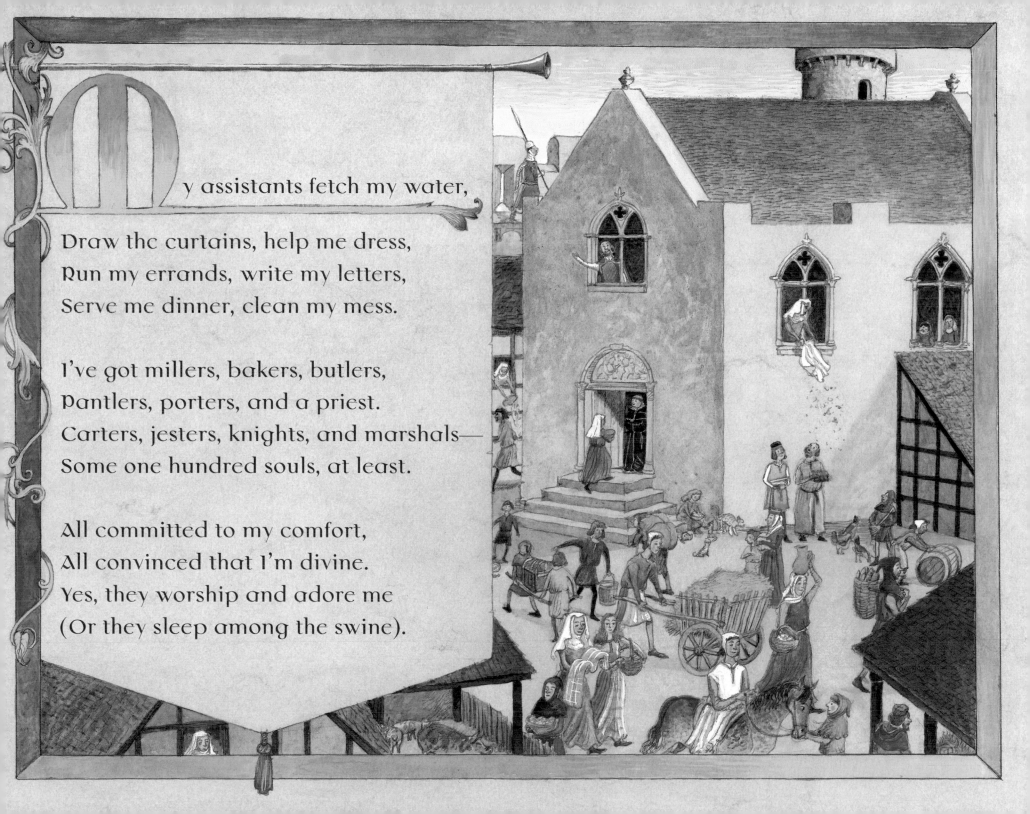

My assistants fetch my water,
Draw the curtains, help me dress,
Run my errands, write my letters,
Serve me dinner, clean my mess.

I've got millers, bakers, butlers,
Pantlers, porters, and a priest.
Carters, jesters, knights, and marshals—
Some one hundred souls, at least.

All committed to my comfort,
All convinced that I'm divine.
Yes, they worship and adore me
(Or they sleep among the swine).

don't need to sweat or toil—
It's the privilege of a lord.
If I ask, the task is finished.
But I must confess . . . I'm *bored*.

he remedy for tedium?
Some merriment, of course!
Steward, plan a tournament!
Herald, find your horse!

teward, plan a tournament?!
The Earl is surely daft!
Though *he* has countless servants,
I am vastly understaffed,
Overworked, and truly weary
Of his constant recreation
(Oh, how I'd love a nice massage
and several weeks' vacation!).

THE STEWARD

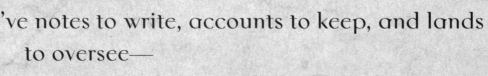

I've notes to write, accounts to keep, and lands
to oversee—
Far too many things to do without this revelry.

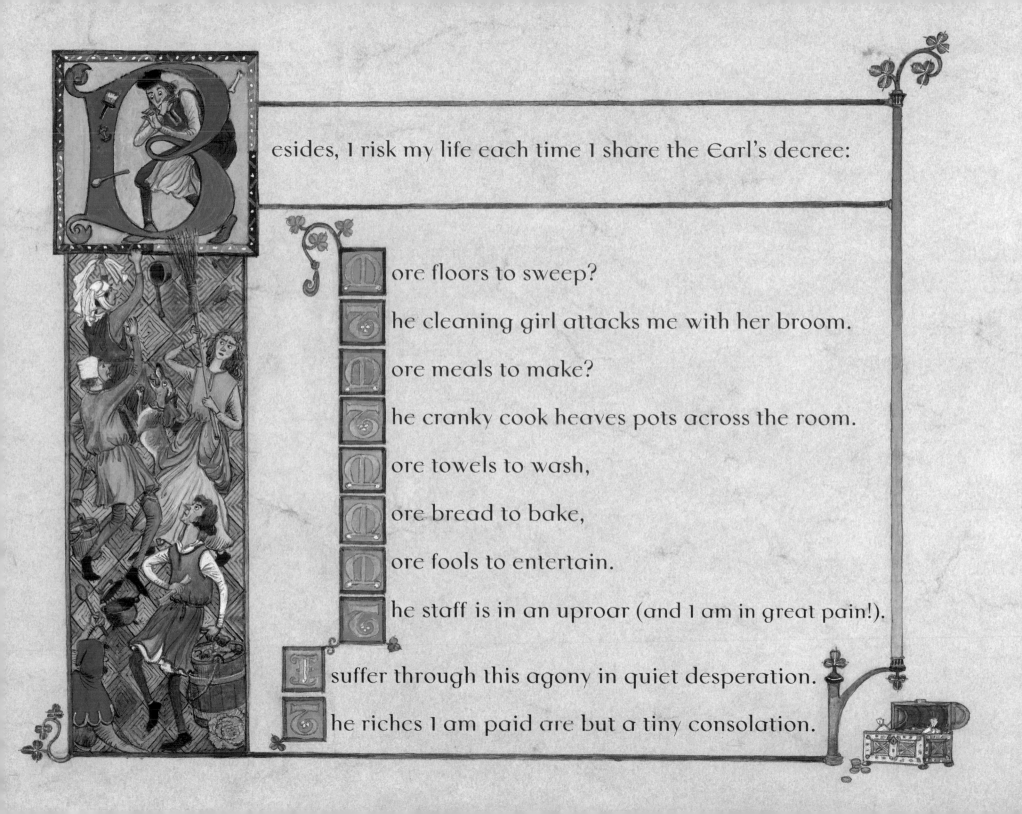

Besides, I risk my life each time I share the Earl's decree:

More floors to sweep?

The cleaning girl attacks me with her broom.

More meals to make?

The cranky cook heaves pots across the room.

More towels to wash,

More bread to bake,

More fools to entertain.

The staff is in an uproar (and I am in great pain!).

I suffer through this agony in quiet desperation.

The riches I am paid are but a tiny consolation.

THE HERALD

Oh, the hardships I endure
Upon these mucky, winding roads!
Slowed by farmers herding cattle,
Tired merchants with their loads,
Troupes of acrobats and minstrels,
Barking dogs and dancing bears,
Wealthy barons with their servants,
Scores of peasants off to fairs.

Robbers hover in the forest.
Wild animals attack.
Steady rain turns roads to rivers.
Constant riding hurts my back.

hen the night falls, all the finest
sleep in downy castle beds,

hile the lesser knights and nobles
find an inn to rest their heads.

s for me, I'm in a stable, bumping elbows, knocking knees—
Stuck with ten pathetic travelers, twenty rats, and countless fleas.

here's no point in my complaining; if the lord decrees, I go.
No matter if there's scorching heat or several feet of snow.
He doesn't care a whit about my constant tribulation,
But risks my life and limb to send another invitation:

A Feast at Daftwood Castle—
Lords and Ladies, come and dine!
We'll keep you fed and entertained
And plied with ale and wine.

We promise jousts and dancing
(And perhaps a messy brawl).
A guarantee of revelry—
Come join us, one and all!

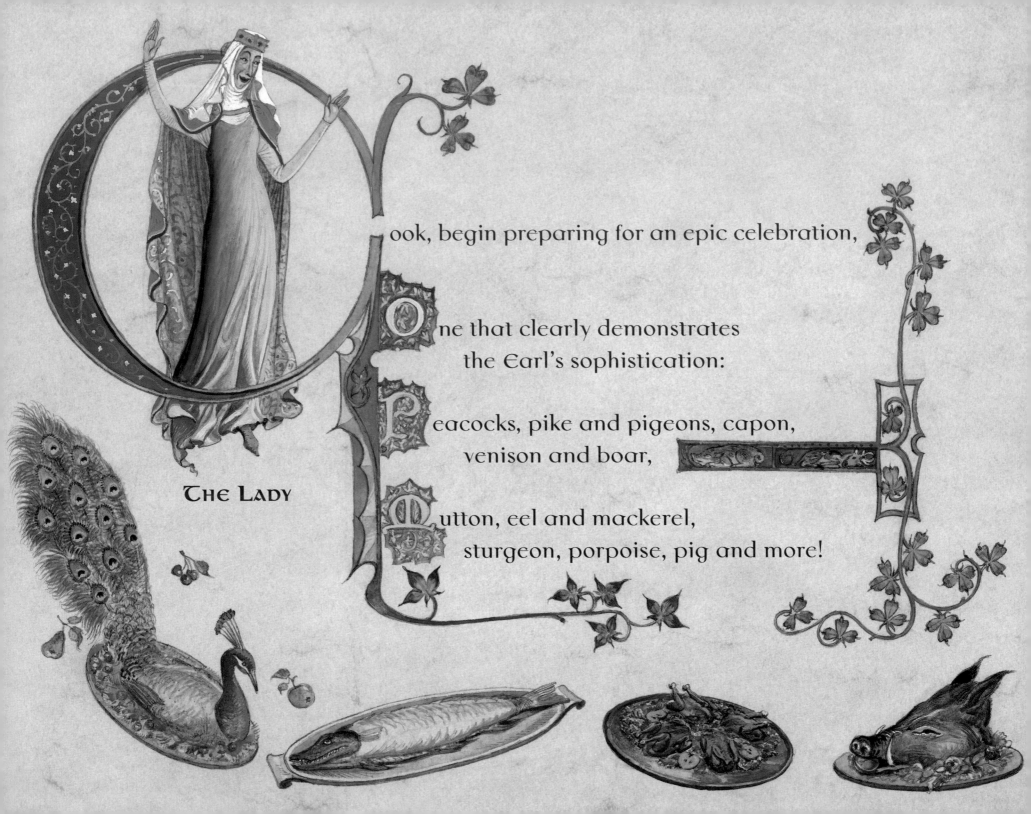

THE LADY

Cook, begin preparing for an epic celebration,

One that clearly demonstrates the Earl's sophistication:

Peacocks, pike and pigeons, capon, venison and boar,

Mutton, eel and mackerel, sturgeon, porpoise, pig and more!

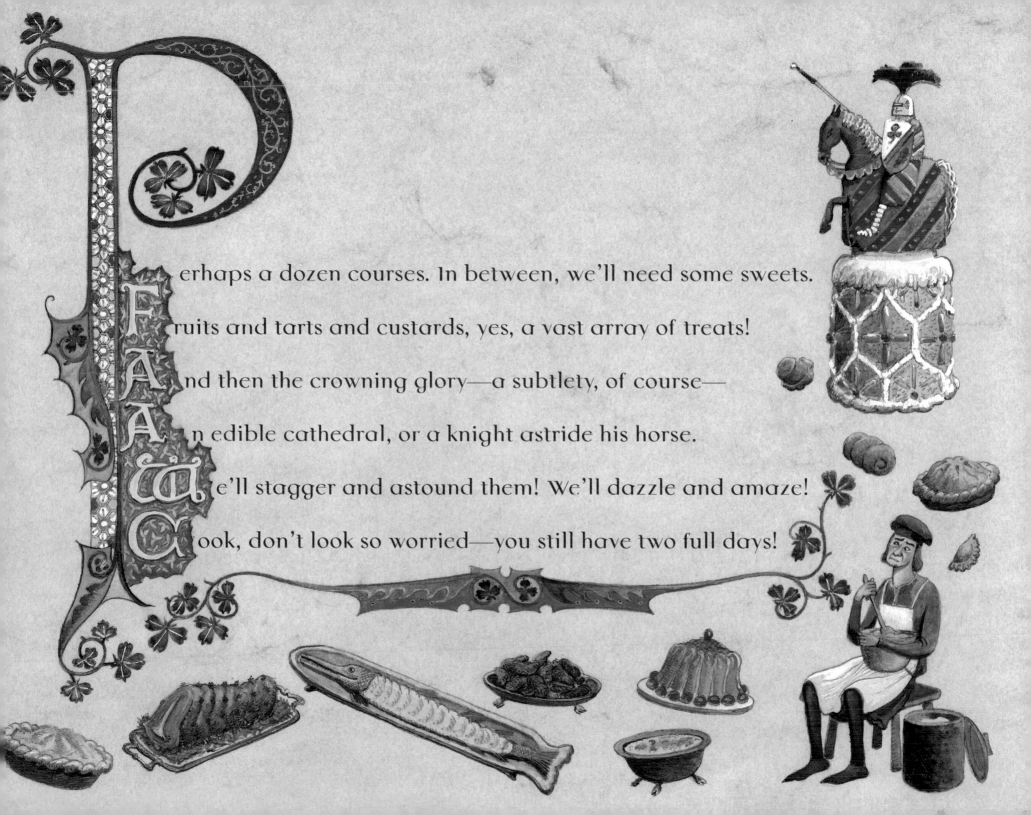

Perhaps a dozen courses. In between, we'll need some sweets.

Fruits and tarts and custards, yes, a vast array of treats!

And then the crowning glory—a subtlety, of course—

An edible cathedral, or a knight astride his horse.

We'll stagger and astound them! We'll dazzle and amaze!

Look, don't look so worried—you still have two full days!

The Cook

have no fresh capon. No porpoise or eel.
No sumptuous roast for a memorable meal.
Still I must follow the Lady's command.
A feast in two days? I'll use what's on hand:

Gizzards and livers and kidneys and feet—
Grind it up well into mystery meat.

ind it with egg, mix it with spice,

Throw in some currants and mustard and rice.

Drop it in stews, bake it in pies,

Roll it in balls (or some other disguise).

Toss on some flowers, gild it with gold.

Present it with antlers or feathers. Be bold!

A fine work of art to fill them with awe—

So what if it's cold, or the meat is still raw?

THE CLEANING SERVANT

Prepare the Great Hall—
The banquet's tonight!
Arrange the old trestles;
Drape them in white.

The goblets must sparkle.
The silver must shine.
Oh no, dear—don't wash them!
Some spit will do fine.

Leave the old dog waste and bones on the floor.
Forget all those meat scraps (we'll soon have some more).
Pile on rushes to cover the grime;
Hide the foul odors with heather and thyme.

catter the rats. Now it's perfectly clean—
Or at least good enough; we're not serving the Queen!

The Gong Farmer

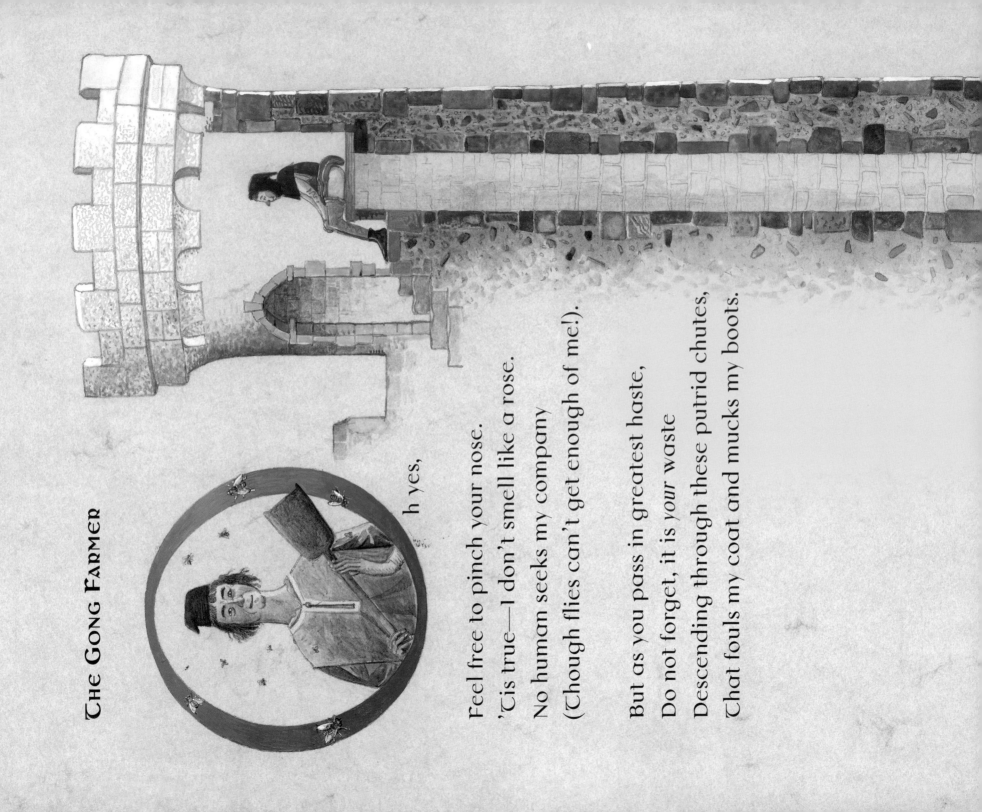

h yes,

Feel free to pinch your nose.
'Tis true—I don't smell like a rose.
No human seeks my company
(Though flies can't get enough of me!).

But as you pass in greatest haste,
Do not forget, it is *your* waste
Descending through these putrid chutes,
That fouls my coat and mucks my boots.

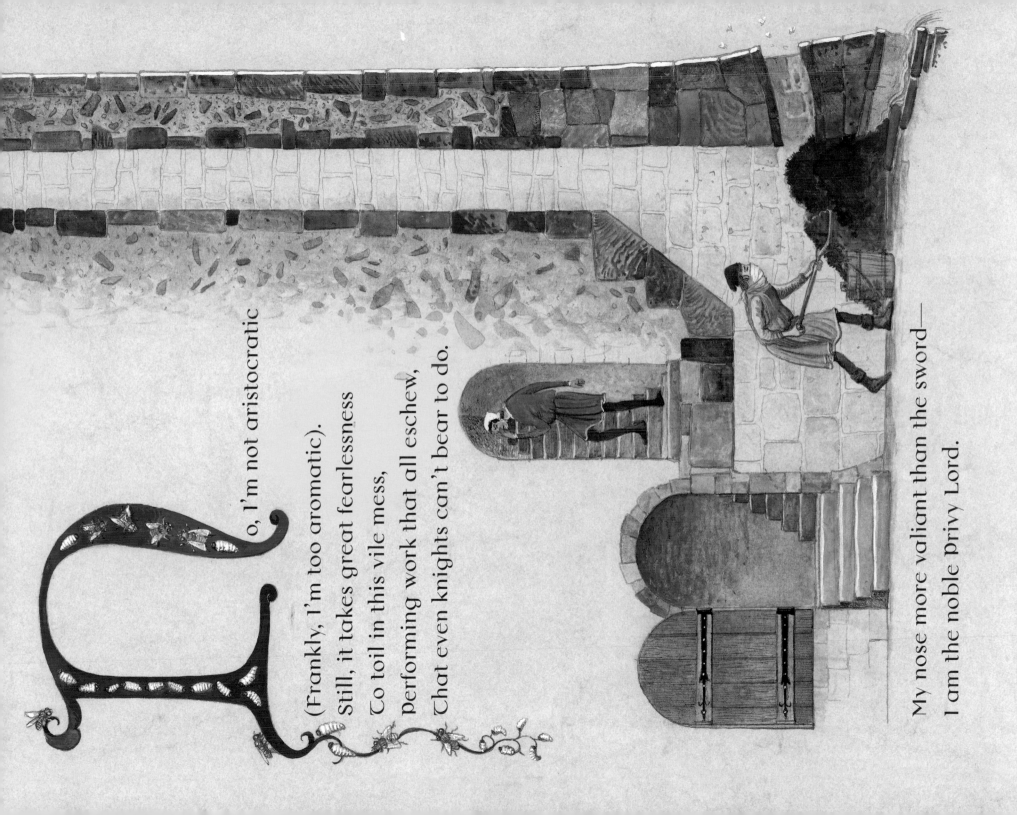

N o, I'm not aristocratic

(Frankly, I'm too aromatic).

Still, it takes great fearlessness

To toil in this vile mess,

Performing work that all eschew,

That even knights can't bear to do.

My nose more valiant than the sword—

I am the noble privy Lord.

THE KNIGHT

ong leather stockings, then mail over that.
A doublet, an aketon, a thick, padded hat.
A hauberk so hot, I am certain to melt.
Plates and a surcoat, gauntlets and belt.

A coif made of metal. A helm with a crest.
Surely this suit was intended in jest!
With holes for my mouth, and slits for my eyes,
I'd gladly go naked and forfeit the prize.

I see little, hear nothing, itch and perspire.
I pray I don't rust before I retire.

The Squire

O h, the glory
    of being a knight!
Defender of Virtue;
    Protector of Right.
Chivalrous, daring,
    prepared for a fight!
I'll be such a glorious knight!

The Knight

O h, the joy
    of jousting in June!
Hearing my name
    in a troubadour's tune.
Racing my steed
    while the fine ladies swoon—
How they worship the noble knight!

The Joust

The Spectator

Oh, the drudge of
    watching these brutes,
Charge at each other
    in ludicrous suits.
I'd rather be pelted
    with moldering fruits,
Than cheer for the boorish knight.

The Healer

Oh, the burden
    of healing this fool—
The strength of a boar,
    the brains of a mule.
Instead of a joust,
    have a thumb-wrestling duel,
And spare me from nursing this knight.

THE SUITOR

y conduct is impeccable; my manners, very fine.
I do not scratch my fleas or pet the canines when I dine.
I swallow all my food before I take another bite.
I belch, but not *too* loudly, for it would not be polite.

I do not ask my host what sort of meat is in the pie.
I drink my soup without removing rodent hair or fly.

would not use the tablecloth to clean my runny nose—
Oh no! I use my hand, of course, then wipe it on my clothes.

I take great care to aim below the table when I spit.
I entertain the ladies with my eloquence and wit.
In summary (as all can see), I'm gracious, charming, wise,
Valiant, poised, and modest; as a husband, quite a prize.

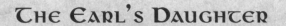

Yet another dreadful suitor at another dreary feast. Evidently I am destined to be married to a beast.

ne is old, another ugly, and a third inclined to drool.
One's a drunkard, one's a braggart; every one of
    them, a fool.

They slurp and gulp and slobber; they jabber without cease.
Spare me from this torture! Let me eat a meal in peace!
Their boasts of jousts and battlefields are utterly inane
(It's clear they use their swords because they have so little brain).

t fourteen, I should not be forced to marry some buffoon.
If I were queen, I'd banish all these dimwits to the moon.

THE JESTER

he trumpets sound! The guests sit down.

The grand procession starts.

Servants carry platters piled with meat and pies and tarts.

The minstrels sing, the jugglers dance,

And I, of course, amuse.

Exciting? Yes! But very tame compared to what ensues:

ord Fleming bumps a squire's hand.
The squire's knife takes flight.
It skims the Earl of Croton's ear, and pokes a drunken knight.

n accident! But nonetheless,
It sparks a nasty brawl—
The knights turn over tables, knock the candles off the wall.

The subsequent inferno
Lights Lord Remington's new coat.
He strips himself completely then dives,
    shrieking, in the moat.

The Duchess cries, "Invasion!"
    (She's dotty as a loon),
    Then climbs atop a table
        waving torch and serving spoon.

Combine a feast with fire,
    Add some knights and too much ale—
    It's a recipe for bedlam
        on a monumental scale.

nd very entertaining (to this audience, at least).

They cheer and dance for hours, then continue with their feast.

The Following Day

gaze at their waters like fine works of art.
Refer to my books and astrology chart.
I pose rather thoughtfully, mumble and pace.
Adopt a concerned, and yet scholarly, face.

scan them for lesions, poke them for tumors,
Prescribe a few herbs to balance the humors.
If, in three days, they're still gripped with pain,
I visit again to open a vein.

The Doctor

he source of their illness?
A monkey could guess:
They stuff themselves silly and drink to excess.
But it is my duty to see them to health—
And, frankly, it adds to my burgeoning wealth!

THE EARL

The servants look exhausted;
The guests, unkempt and pale.
The larders are all empty;
There's not a drop of ale.

The grounds are a disaster.
The castle is a mess—
There's every indication that
our fete was a success!

How do we top this triumph?
Some merriment, of course!

teward, plan a tournament!
Herald, find your horse!

AUTHOR'S NOTE

Several years ago, I became curious about life in the Middle Ages. In particular, I wondered what it might have been like to live in a castle at that time. As I focused my research on thirteenth-century England, distinct characters began to emerge in my mind: a wealthy but dim-witted lord; his overworked steward; his beleaguered staff; his intelligent daughter, forced to endure the attentions of various unappealing suitors. These characters are fictional, of course, and I've taken some poetic license for the sake of humor and drama (for example, the planning and execution of the tournament is compressed into a matter of days). Still, in writing these poems, I've tried to give a fairly accurate glimpse of castle life during this period.

Cast of Characters

A wealthy lord like THE EARL OF DAFTWOOD might live in a huge castle (or castles!), with vast amounts of land and more than one hundred servants.

THE STEWARD had many responsibilities, including managing the lord's estates. As the most important member of the staff, he was very well paid.

 Among other duties, THE HERALD delivered messages for the lord. Roads were bumpy and very crowded, and traveling by horseback was difficult and often dangerous. Except for the very wealthy, overnight accommodations were likely to be uncomfortable—and possibly filthy and rat-infested.

 THE LADY of the castle often supervised large banquets, which were a good opportunity to impress guests with the family's wealth and excellent taste. Such a feast might last for hours, with many different courses and sweets served in between. A *subtlety* was a particularly elaborate edible creation shaped like a person, animal, building—anything at all—designed to surprise and entertain guests.

 THE COOK used nearly every part of an animal; very little was wasted. While the dishes might look stunning—decorated with flowers, gold, feathers, and antlers, among other things—they were often undercooked or cold by the time they arrived at the table.

Although THE CLEANING SERVANT and crew worked hard to prepare the castle for a feast, standards of cleanliness were quite different from today's. Dogs were welcome in the Great Hall, and their waste might be left on the floor alongside bones, food droppings, grease, and spilled wine and ale. All of this would be covered with leaves or straw, with fragrant herbs added to hide the smell.

THE GONG FARMER had perhaps the worst job in the castle: cleaning out the waste from the *garderobe* or *privy*—the medieval equivalent of the bathroom. There were no flushing toilets in the Middle Ages. Rather, the waste fell down a long chute into the moat or a pit.

THE KNIGHT wore many layers of protective clothing to prepare for a *joust*, a form of entertainment in which knights on horseback charged at each other and tried to topple their opponents with a lance. The *doublet*, an undershirt, and *aketon*, a padded undercoat, were worn beneath a *hauberk*, a coat of *chain mail* comprised of metal rings linked together. A chain mail *coif*, or hood, and a metal *helm*, or helmet, was worn on the head. The armor was heavy (sometimes weighing more than sixty pounds!), hot, and uncomfortable. Despite all this protection, injuries were common.

THE SUITOR, hoping to make a good impression on his host and win the hand of his daughter, followed very strict rules of dining etiquette. Standards have changed considerably since then, and someone following those rules today would be considered very ill-mannered, indeed.

THE DAUGHTER would have had little say in choosing her husband, as marriages typically were arranged by parents, usually for financial benefit. Girls could be married as young as twelve years old, and most were married by their late teens.

THE JESTER was one of many performers who might entertain at a banquet, along with musicians, jugglers, and acrobats. Some were traveling entertainers; others were part of a wealthy lord's staff.

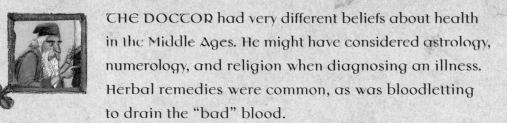

THE DOCTOR had very different beliefs about health in the Middle Ages. He might have considered astrology, numerology, and religion when diagnosing an illness. Herbal remedies were common, as was bloodletting to drain the "bad" blood.

Acknowledgments

Many thanks to Rebecca Barnhouse, Professor of English at Youngstown State University, for her generosity and thoughtfulness in reviewing the manuscript. As a teacher of medieval literature, and an author as well, her insights were invaluable. Professor Barnhouse also referred me to Norman Hinton, Emeritus Professor of English from the University of Illinois-Springfield, who reviewed the manuscript and offered additional comments. I am grateful for their expertise and kindness.—L.A.

I would like to thank Susan and Leslie for obtaining visual reference material. —S.D.S.

To Sally Kahler Phillips, friend extraordinaire

—L.A.

To Liz, my favorite medievalist

—S.D.S.

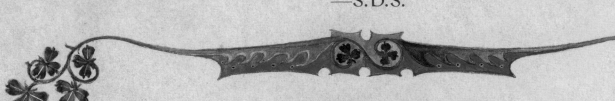

Text copyright © 2009 by Linda Ashman

Illustrations copyright © 2009 by S. D. Schindler

Flash Point is an imprint of Roaring Brook Press,

a division of Holtzbrinck Publishing Holdings Limited Partnership

175 Fifth Avenue, New York, New York 10010

www.roaringbrookpress.com

Distributed in Canada by H. B. Fenn and Company, Ltd.

Cataloging-in-Publication Data is on file at the Library of Congress

ISBN-13: 978-1-59643-155-3

ISBN-10: 1-59643-155-5

Roaring Brook Press books are available for special promotions and premiums.

For details, contact: Director of Special Markets, Holtzbrinck Publishers.

Book design by Jennifer Browne

Printed in China

First edition April 2009

1 3 5 7 9 10 8 6 4 2

6-09 d